UNION WITH ROME?

St. Raphael of Brooklyn

The Works
of Saint Raphael of Brooklyn

Volume 1: In Defense of Saint Cyprian

Volume 2: On the Steadfastness of the Orthodox Church

Volume 3: Union with Rome?

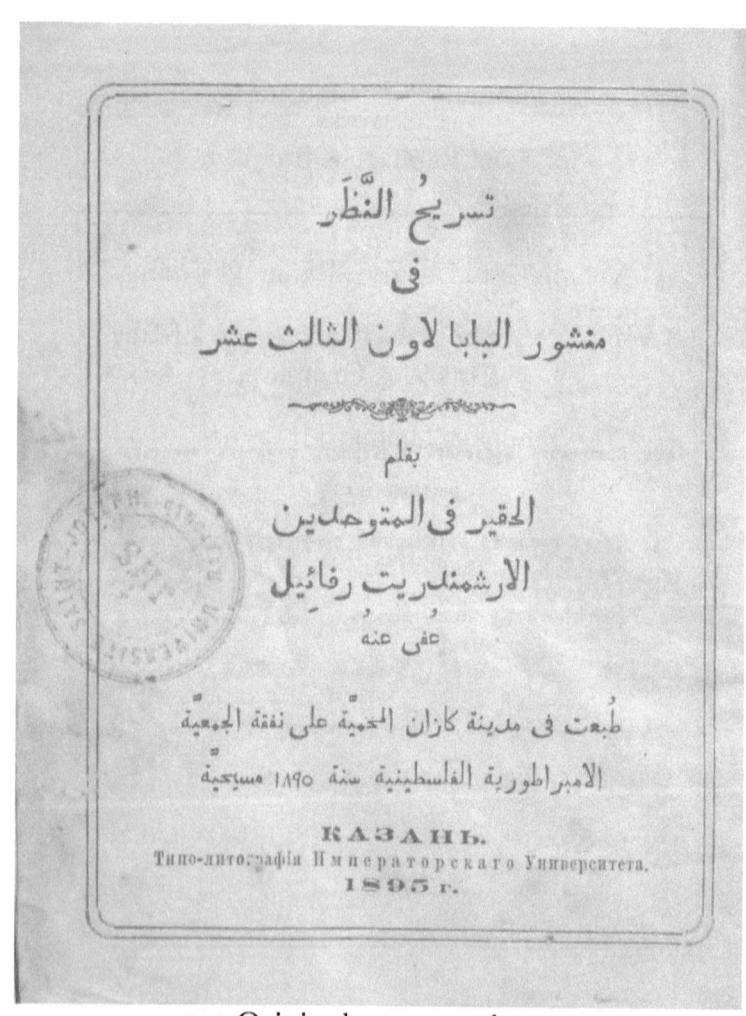

Original cover reads:

Setting our Sights on the Encyclical of Pope Leo XIII by the humble among the Monastics: Archimandrite Raphael. May he be forgiven. Printed in the protected city of Kazan at the expense of the Imperial Palestinian Organization in the year 1895 A.D. KAZAN. Typo-lithography of the Imperial University. 1895.

Union With Rome?

Refuting the Encyclical of Pope Leo XIII

Saint Raphael (Hawaweeny)
Bishop of Brooklyn

Uncut Mountain Press

UNION WITH ROME?
Refuting the Encyclical of Pope Leo XIII

© 2025
Uncut Mountain Press

All rights reserved
under International and Pan-American Copyright Conventions.

uncutmountainpress.com

Special thanks to Maher Salloum.

Originally published in Arabic under the title *Setting our Sights on the Encyclical of Pope Leo XIII* by Kazan Imperial University (1895).

All images are in the public domain unless cited otherwise.

Scriptural quotations are emended to better reflect the original text.

Saint Raphael (Hawaweeny) of Brooklyn, 1860–1915.
Union With Rome? Refuting the Encyclical of Pope Leo XIII—1st ed.

ISBN (softcover): 978-1-63941-081-1
ISBN (ebook): 978-1-63941-083-5

I. Orthodox Christian History
II. Orthodox Christian Ecclesiology

"Let no one imagine that we hold the spirit of fanaticism or the hatred of peace toward the divided Christian churches and their union. On the contrary, the spirit of peace, love, and unity is the spirit of the Orthodox Church, and it spreads it in the hearts and minds of its children from their youth through its Christian teachings and daily and nightly prayers. But we cannot accept a false union such as the one presented to us by Pope Leo XIII..."

— From Part 9

CONTENTS

Introduction: From the Translator **11**

Part 1: The Autumn of Papal Glory **21**

Part 2: Papal Audacity **25**

Part 3: Saint Peter's Relation to the Other Apostles **29**

Part 4: "Thou art Peter..." **35**

Part 5: The Vatican's Deceptive Historical Approach **43**

Part 6: Infallibility **51**

Part 7: The Pope's False Promises **55**

Part 8: The Pope's Lofty Promises **59**

Part 9: Papal Administration **61**

Part 10: Response of Pope Gregory the Great to Patriarch John the Faster **67**

Part 11: The West's Corrupting Influence **71**

St. Raphael of Brooklyn

INTRODUCTION
From the Translator

THE WRITINGS OF SAINT RAPHAEL

The Arabic writings of St. Raphael of Brooklyn are not well known to the English reader. Hundreds of pages of articles and sermons written by St. Raphael were published in the *Word* magazine since it was founded by him in 1905 until his repose in 1915, along with many articles published posthumously. They cover a large variety of dogmatic, scriptural, historical, spiritual, liturgical and pastoral topics. We have been translating selections of these articles at Uncut Mountain Press. Saint Raphael also has writings and translations in Arabic of Church history, apologetics and liturgics, as listed in his life published by Archdeacon Emmanuel Abu Hatab.[1]

---

[1] See "The Affections of the Children toward the Most Benevolent among Hierarchs and most Affectionate among Fathers" (A'watif al abnaa' nah'wa khayr al roo'assaa' wa a'ataf al 'abaa' - عواطف الأبناء نحو خير الرؤساء وأعطف الآباء), Archdeacon Emmanuel Abou Hatab, 1915.

One of these writings is a response by Saint Raphael to an encyclical by pope Leo XIII in 1894[2] where the pope calls the Orthodox Church to be united with Catholicism under his rule. Saint Raphael's response to that encyclical was one of several responses written by the Orthodox (the most important response being the one written by the Orthodox patriarchs of the East in 1895[3]—considered the last document defending the Orthodox Faith against papist heresies jointly written by all Eastern Orthodox patriarchs).

WHO WAS POPE LEO XIII?

Pope Leo XIII (1810–1903) was the successor of Pope Pius IX. He was educated by the Jesuit order and ruled as pope from 1878–1903. He wrote several encyclicals aiming to start a dialogue with the non-Catholics as well as all the world. He is known to be against Freemasonry and secular Liberalism. It is said that he saw a terrifying vision of Satan's evil plans against his church. For instance, he complains in the encyclical about the rise of hatred and dissensions against the Roman church along with the turmoils of revolution in Europe. He claims that the union of the East and West is a way to face these dangers and also to prevent wars. Thus, he invites the churches of the East to be united under his rule. In the encyclical, he reiterates the usual papal claims of their primacy and authority over all the Church using the usual clever language to provide twisted and truncated truths.

---

2 Praeclara Gratulationis Publicae, "The Reunion of Christendom," Pope Leo XIII – 1894. Available here:
https://www.papalencyclicals.net/leo13/l13praec.htm

3 This response is available here: http://orthodoxinfo.com/ecumenism/encyc_1895.aspx

Introduction

THE RESPONSE OF SAINT RAPHAEL OF BROOKLYN

In contrast with the vague language of Pope Leo XIII, Saint Raphael provides clear and firm responses and rebuttals to the claims in the encyclical. No, says Saint Raphael, a union with Rome cannot be established based on falsehoods such as papal primacy and other heresies and fabrications. He focuses on refuting the papal claims of primacy and supremacy over the Church, as well as all arguments used by papal apologists to support these claims, such as the argument of the pope being the successor of Saint Peter the Apostle, and that Saint Peter had authority over all other Apostles. The citations provided by Saint Raphael from the Church Fathers, as well as both eastern and western historians, prove his vast knowledge of Church dogma and history. For instance, he cites historians such as Fleury and Pitzipios who, to our knowledge, have never been explored nor studied in other Orthodox books.

The second part of the response of Saint Raphael focuses on addressing the promises of Pope Leo XIII to the Eastern Orthodox Church should they accept uniting with him. Here, Saint Raphael reminds the pope and warns the Orthodox faithful of the horrific consequence of uniting with the pope. Unfortunately, experience has taught us that we cannot trust any type of assistance that the pope can grant to the Orthodox Church. The west, even before the days of pope Leo XIII, has been corrupted by different Christian-hating ideologies and sects, such as Freemasonry, Socialism, Anarchism, etc. A major reason for the formation of these ideologies is the terrible feudal system governing the papist administration and their legalist theology and indulgences. As for the material goods promised by the pope, these cannot be trusted either, given that the majority of the people in Europe at that time had been living in poverty.

But the greatest danger discussed by Saint Raphael is the creation of Uniatism (e.g. the so-called "Byzantine Catholics") by the pope before the nineteenth century. This brought nothing but division and subjugation of these groups to the papist mentality and institution. Saint Raphael also alludes to the atmosphere of Ecumenism that was created within the Uniate circles in the east. The combination of the "Byzantine," Syriac, Armenian, etc. denominations, who disagree on different matters of faith within themselves as well as with Catholicism, who were proselytized and united under the pope, is the first type of Ecumenism that infested the body of believers in the east and has been intensifying and spread in the west.

Throughout his response, Saint Raphael is eloquent and astute in his analysis and unraveling of the claims of Pope Leo XIII. The pope's encyclical is impressive in its twisting of the facts by mixing truths and falsehoods, and providing half-truths, while using flattering language and words.

THE AUTHENTICITY OF SAINT RAPHAEL'S RESPONSE:

The translator of this book has been interested in Orthodox writings published before the twentieth century. While reading the life of Saint Raphael referenced above, we came to learn about the titles of books written by Saint Raphael. One of them is the very famous Great Euchologion that Saint Raphael collected from several Greek and Russian resources and made available in Arabic. Another title that stood out is the current book which title rhymes in Arabic "tasree'h al nadh'ar fi manshoor al baba Lawon al th'aleth' a'shar - تسريح النظر في منشور البابا لاون الثالث عشر, which literally translates into "Setting the sight in the encyclical of Pope Leo XIII." This title seemed intriguing to us in the beginning, but after learning about the encyclical of Pope Leo XIII and the reaction to it of the Patriarchs of the East, we became quite

Introduction

curious as to what a Saint of the Orthodox Church has to say about it.

Our research for this book started with available online search engines. We discovered that it was actually a book, not a manuscript, and that a copy existed, ironically, in Saint Joseph University, a Jesuit institution in Lebanon. While such a book could be found in other libraries, we focused our efforts to access the old library of Saint Joseph University and obtain a copy. After several attempts, we were successful in obtaining a PDF copy with the help of faithful Orthodox friends in Lebanon.

As the Arabic text suggests, the text was composed in the Theological Academy of Kazan in Russia in December of 1894 and published in 1895, i.e., very soon after the publication of the papal encyclical and just before Saint Raphael arrived to North America. At that time, he was still an Archimandrite, as stated on the book's cover page. The text style and cited references prove that the response is written in Arabic by Saint Raphael himself, not in another language and then translated into Arabic. First, the style of the text matches the style used by Saint Raphael in his thesis at Halki Theological Academy. Some cited works are also the same in both Saint Raphael's thesis and response to Pope Leo XIII. Second, the Arabic text contains Arabic expressions and a verse of Arabic poetry suggesting that it is originally written in Arabic.

While translating the text, we encountered names of authors (historians, theologians, etc.) and of works of theology and history that were transcribed into Arabic. It was not an easy task to discover the names of these authors and works. But with the help of Artificial Intelligence (AI) solutions such as Copilot and Gemini, we were able to not only discover nearly all of these names, but also to find the original quotations. We were delighted in such an effective use of the rising AI engines and we pray that they will be used in a constructive manner for the benefit of the Church and the spreading of the Orthodox Faith.

THE RELEVANCE OF SAINT RAPHAEL'S RESPONSE FOR OUR TIME:

When working on this text, we were tempted to think that this response of Saint Raphael to the encyclical of pope Leo XIII in 1894 is nothing but a mere dwelling in the past and its glories, and that it is not applicable to our days. On the contrary, while examining the events of our days, it is apparent that we are facing many of the same challenges and circumstances of the late nineteenth century. As we say "history repeats itself."[4] Indeed, efforts are likewise underway today that serve to subjugate the Orthodox Church and Faith to Papalism, but with much greater subtlety and refinement, with machinations ranging from political pressure to emotional sentimentality and cultural assimilation.

On one hand, the powers against Christianity are increasing in the world and we need to unite to be able to confront them—a major theme that is often raised. At first glance, one would logically reason that this is true. As we can see all over the world, there are real attempts to normalize practices that are against Christianity in our churches, such as sexual promiscuity and license, abortion, homosexuality, female priesthood, gender re-definition, and more. On the other hand, voices are demanding the union of the churches to face world poverty and other economical problems. Uniting with the pope seems a viable solution to all these challenges, given the influence and power that the

---

4 As we reached the final editing stages of this book, Pope Leo XIV was elected. Is it a mere coincidence or providence that he is the Leo directly after Pope Leo XIII, the subject of this book?

pope has on the Western world. One can also reason that the pope and other voices encouraging such a union have good and honest intentions.

And yet, as Saint Raphael responded then to similar claims, we likewise respond today in the negative, as this is not how a true union could be accomplished. Even if the pope and others have good intentions, church union cannot be established under the pretext of "love" as it is preached today. Union cannot be established outside the truth of the One Holy, Catholic, Orthodox, and Apostolic Church, co-existing or being mixed up with the heretical teachings still clung to by the papacy.

An even more subtle and dangerous disease facing the Orthodox Church at this time is the danger of Ecumenism. As mentioned previously, Saint Raphael alludes to Ecumenism as it appeared among Uniates who sought to preserve their [eastern] beliefs and practices while uniting themselves to the pope (see Part 9). This is exactly the type of Ecumenism that we see nowadays. As Elder Athanasios Mitilinaios describes it: "What are you, Protestant? What am I, Orthodox? What are you, Roman Catholic? Look, let's just forget our differences; let's put them aside. Let's just forget our histories and what brought us here. All that matters is the present and a peaceful future. 'Love is what counts. Love is what's important.'"[5] Specific to Papalism, the role of Uniatism in the bolstering of ecumenistic efforts is quite obvious today. Eastern Catholics, themselves, openly claim they are the "bridge" between Rome and Orthodoxy.[6] Our present publication refutes all these claims, hence, it is not a mere dwelling in the past but rather addresses

---

[5] Elder Athanasios Mitilinaios, *Revelation: The Seven Golden Lampstands*, trans. Constantine Zalalas (Dunlap, CA: Zoe Press, 2016), p. 137.

[6] See for example: https://melkite.org/faith/faith-worship/introduction

contemporary dangers against which the Orthodox Church must stand firm, offering a clear exposition of the Faith.

By near-universal agreement, we are quickly approaching the *eschaton* and the fulfillment of the Lord's prophetic words for the last Christians. We can expect that the war waged by Ecumenism against the Orthodox Church and the Holy Fathers will intensify, becoming more refined and difficult to discern and confront. It is, thus, our hope that this confession of the Orthodox Faith will contribute to the sharpening of the faithful's discernment of spirits and watchfulness.

The twentieth and twenty-first centuries have witnessed several unfortunate events and attempts to cause divisions in the Body of the Church. This should not cause us to fall into despair because Christ keeps sending us Saints and defenders of the Orthodox Faith, such as Saint Raphael of Brooklyn. May we stand steadfast in our Faith through their intercessions, and may we receive the Great Mercy of our Lord, God and Savior Jesus Christ, to Whom belongs all glory and worship, now and ever and unto the ages of ages. Amen.

Introduction

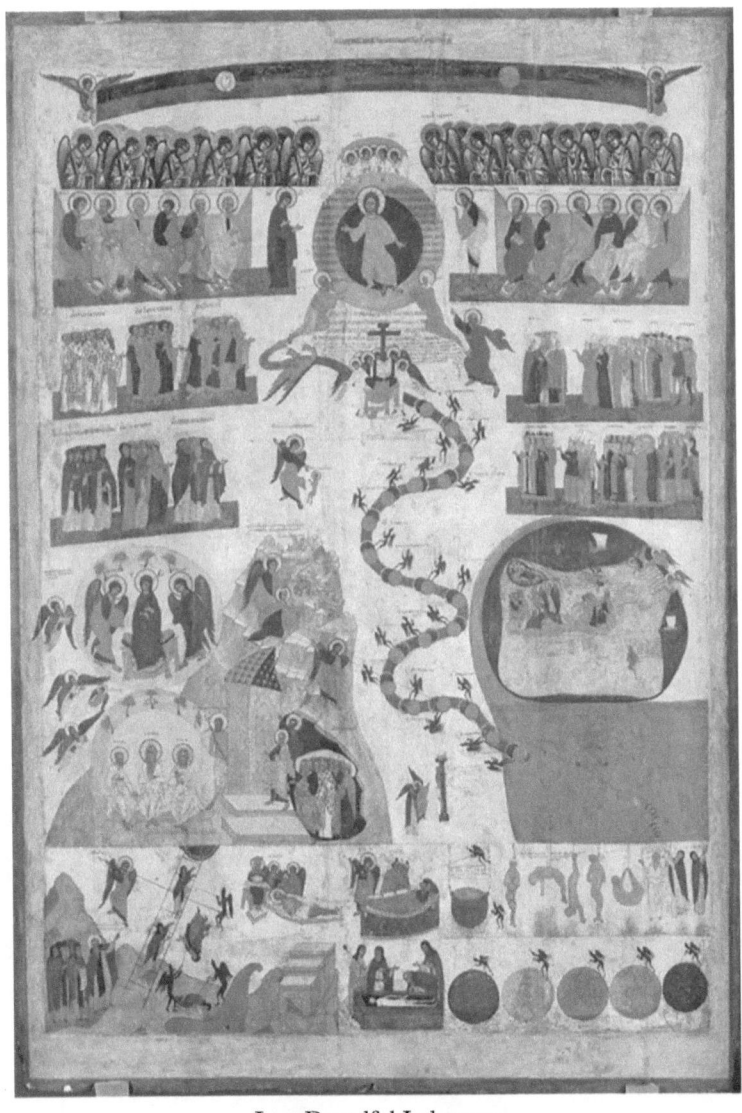

Last Dreadful Judgment
16th century, Novgorod (Russia)

St. Raphael of Brooklyn

PART 1

The Autumn of Papal Glory

There is no doubt that our current age, compared to all previous ages, is the one with the most need to unite the diffused powers of the Christian world and to associate them together, so that Christians, united under the banner of the glorious Holy Cross, are able to repel the vehement enemies of the Christian faith—by whom I mean the evil athcists: groups of materialists, socialists, nihilists, anarchists, and those like them, among the children of the papist church and all Protestant sects—who began in recent times spreading the teachings that God handed down with authority, not according to current scientific truths but according to weak imaginary assumptions. Thus, they began troubling, with their terrible teachings, the conscience of the simple faithful, and disturbed, by their horrible acts, the serene and healthy life of the people, especially in the West, where the papist church, being alienated from the remaining Eastern churches of Christ, became unable to repel the arrows of the enemies of the Christian religion. On the contrary, it brought hatred and abhorrence upon itself from many of its own children, let alone the remaining non-papist Christians, due to its several heresies, its many innovations, and the gross claims of its leaders that are at odds with the spirit of Christian teaching and incompatible with the Apostolic Traditions, and increased the malice and defiance of the enemies of the faith and religion, and it thereby dug its own grave.

And no matter how much the co-papists, of all their tints and parties, strive to show off that their church, under the mercy of its visible head, is still flourishing and glowing, it is nevertheless more like an autumn tree shedding its leaves under a soft breeze. For how many hundreds, rather thousands and millions, have separated up until now from the papist church since its schism from the Orthodox Church of Christ? And what is the reason for the separation of these millions from the papist church other than its strange heresies and many innovations in most dogmas, rituals, and old Christian practices? Was not the heresy of indulgence bonds the main reason for the separation of the Protestants? And was not the heresy of papal infallibility what recently alienated tens of hundreds from the papist church? And was not the bold claim of its leaders in the right of authority and headship over all the Church what deprived it from the grace of union with the other Orthodox churches of Christ, and recently brought it to fall and decay?

But despite all this, instead of abandoning all its innovative teachings that became a reason, first, to separate itself from the Eastern Church, and, second, to alienate from it millions in the Western countries, and return to its status before the schism and unite with the other Orthodox churches and unite to itself all Protestant and Catholic denominations, we see that papist church, conversely, still insists on these heinous teachings, in addition to innovating, age after age, other new teachings more heinous than the first! So, is it not right for us to say, in this case, that all hopes of uniting the Eastern churches with the papist church are vain no matter how frequently the popes of Rome utter expressions of love and words of flattery toward the Eastern

1. The Autumn of Papal Glory

faithful in their letters and encyclicals, as long as they insist on the teachings contrary to the spirit of Scriptures and Tradition that they innovated in the foundations of faith and religion?

But let us read now through the encyclical of Pope Leo XIII where he specifically invites the Orthodox churches of the East to unite with the papist church, hoping that he commits therein at least to abandon the innovative papist teachings post-schism which, as we said, are the strongest hindrances to unity.

Exile of Adam and Eve from Paradise

Pope Leo XIII

PART 2

Papal Audacity

Before anything else, and after what we have always been reading in the writings and editorials of Catholic newspapers about the sad situation of the "Vatican prisoner,"[7] we were hoping to hear in this encyclical the voice of an actual sad, wretched, weak, and miserable prisoner. But these hopes were dashed to the ground as soon as we looked at the title of the encyclical that the pope starts with this expression that is full of pride and arrogance: "from our holy master, by God's help, Pope Leo XIII, greetings and peace in the Lord to the kings and all peoples"![8] This is the speech not of a confined prisoner, but of an ultimate master who does not reckon daringly to address "the kings and all peoples" and invite them to listen to his sayings and

---

[7] Translator's note: This is a surname that Pope Pius IX, the predecessor of Pope Leo XIII, took upon himself after revolts against him.

[8] Translator's note: The encyclical of Pope Leo the XIII along with its title can be found in Latin here: https://www.vatican.va/content/leo-xiii/la/apost_letters/documents/hf_l-xiii_apl_18940620_praeclara-gratulationis.html

words. And what is astonishing in this expression[9] is that it implies that the encyclical is not written by the pope, but by somebody else on behalf of the pope, since the following expressions in the encyclical show that the author is the pope himself. Perhaps this is also among the strange habits of the popes! But what is more astonishing than this is what the pope calls himself in the beginning of the encyclical, that he is the "vicar of Almighty God on earth"! But if we disregard this expression, due to its highly blasphemous content since it indicates that the pope shares divine power with God Almighty, we wonder when did God establish the pope of Rome as His vicar on earth? If God Almighty wanted to establish to Himself a vicar on earth, He would have revealed such great ordeal to His Holy Church in His revered Book, at least in order to preserve it from the evil conflicts and schisms which resulted from the claims of the popes of Rome that they are established by God as primates over all the Church, as Pope Leo XIII himself affirms in his encyclical where he says, "the principal subject of their contention [i.e. the differences of the Orthodox of the East] with us is the dogma of the primacy of the great Roman pontiff." So if this is the case, which expression in Holy Scripture witnesses, or at least hints, to give the bishops of Rome the right of primacy over all the Church, upon which the Westerners built castles and high places to the point of making the pope the visible head of the Church, and the deputy of Christ, and the vicar of God on earth, who holds the keys of paradise and hell, and the infallible one? If we want to search through all the expressions in Holy Scripture, we would be worn out searching for even one word that supports the claim of the popes of Rome in the right of primacy over all the Church. But Pope Leo XIII saves us

---

9   Translator's note: It seems that St. Raphael is referring to the opening expression of the encyclical "from our holy master" which implies that it is not the pope himself who wrote it.

2. Papal Audacity 27

the burden of this search, for he points us in his encyclical to that expression in Holy Scripture that supports, according to his claim, the right of primacy over all the Church, that is: "you are Peter, and on this rock I will build My church" (Matthew 16:18)!

But let us look first if Christ the Lord, by saying this to Peter, really made him the only foundation of the Church, and thereby a primate over the rest of the apostles, and a head of all the church, and His vicar of earth, as the papists claim; and second, if we assume that Peter received these privileges, rights, and features from the Lord Christ, by what right do the popes of Rome attribute them to themselves?

St. John Chrysostom

PART 3

Saint Peter's Relation to the Other Apostles

Concerning the first claim of the papists, we say that no rational man carefully reads that gospel verse, with what precedes and what follows it, without understanding it, as the greatest Church fathers understood it, that this saying of the Lord is the response to the confession of Peter the Apostle that Christ the Lord is the living Son of God. Thus, the rock is equivalent to the confession and faith in Jesus Christ as the living Son of God, not to the person of Peter himself. As such, Saint John Chrysostom says in his Homily 54 on Matthew: "Upon this rock, that is, on this faith and this confession." Likewise, Blessed Augustine, whom the Latins consider one the greatest defenders of all the dogmas of Rome, says the following in his interpretation of this saying of the Lord to Peter: "Thou art Peter, Christ says, and on this rock that you confessed, i.e. you knew through your confession—You are Christ the Son of the living God—I build My Church. I build you on Myself, not Myself [i.e. My Body, My Church] do I build upon you. For those who wanted to build people on the foundation of people used to say: 'I am of Apollos, or I am of Cephas' [i.e. Peter, 1 Corinthians 1:12]." All celebrated fathers and teachers of the Holy Church, both Eastern and Western, understood and interpreted this Gospel verse likewise.

But still, if we understand this verse literally and considered that the word 'rock' refers to the person of Peter himself, nevertheless, the builder is Christ (see also 1 Corinthians 3:9) not Peter, and the Church is the Church of Christ, not the Church of Peter, because the Lord did not say, "You build your church," but He said, "I build my Church." In this sense, we see that Holy Scriptures call all the apostles, even all the true believers in Jesus Christ, rocks and stones and foundations upon which the Church of Christ is built, where Christ is its chosen precious cornerstone i.e. its only primary foundation. As such, the Apostle Paul writes to the Ephesians: "Now, therefore, you are no longer strangers and foreigners, but fellow citizens with the saints and members of the household of God, having been built on the foundation of the apostles and prophets, Jesus Christ Himself being the chief cornerstone" (Ephesians 2:19-21). Likewise, the Apostle Peter himself says in his first Epistle "...you also, as living stones, are being built up a spiritual house, a holy priesthood, to offer up spiritual sacrifices acceptable to God through Jesus Christ. Therefore it is also contained in the Scripture, 'Behold, I lay in Zion a chief cornerstone, elect, precious, And he who believes on Him will by no means be put to shame.' Therefore, to you who believe, He is precious; but to those who are disobedient, 'The stone which the builders rejected Has become the chief cornerstone'" (1 Peter 2:5-7). And the Book of Revelation says: "...the wall of the city [i.e. the Church] had twelve foundations, and on them were the names of the twelve apostles of the Lamb" (Revelation 21:14). Hence, it becomes clearly evident that the Church of Christ is built not on the foundation of Peter alone, but on the foundation of all twelve apostles, and that the foundation of all these foundations is the Lord Jesus Christ alone, as the Apostle

3. St. Peter's Relation to Other Apostles

Paul witnesses in his First Epistle to the Corinthians where he expressly says, "For no other foundation can anyone lay than that which is laid, which is Jesus Christ" (1 Corinthians 3:11), thus, the only head of the Church is neither Peter nor any other apostle, but the Lord Jesus Christ Himself as the Apostle Paul also confirms when he says: "He [i.e. God] put all things under His feet (i.e. the feet of Jesus Christ), and gave Him to be head over all things to the church, which is His body [not Peter's body], the fullness of Him who fills all in all" (Ephesians 1:22-23 cf. 5:23).

Not to mention that the papists' claim that Jesus Christ gave the Apostle Peter some special authority over the other apostles is contrary to the spirit of Christian teachings and inconsistent with the words of the Gospel. For if we carefully read the Holy Gospel, we see that the Lord Christ in all His teachings, commandments, and orders to His apostles always warns them against the spirit of authority and lust of power, and reveals to them that there should not be among them firsts and lasts, precedents and followers, principals and subordinates, powerful and despised, not even to be called teacher and lord, but they all have to be equal among each other as brethren and serve each other with humility and love according to the example He showed them Himself—their Divine Teacher and Lord (see Matthew 20:20-28, Mark 10:42-45, Luke 22:23-27 and John 13:13-16). Actually, we see that all the apostles, in all their works and sayings, followed the example of their divine Master and Teacher, our Lord and God Jesus Christ. They never fulfilled any important work nor issued any order except by mutual agreement among themselves, such as appointing Matthias to be an apostle in place of Judas Iscariot (Acts 1:23-26), electing seven deacons (Acts 6:2-6), solving the question of circumcision (Acts 15), etc., while the Apostle Peter, in all his meetings with the rest of the apostles, was considered a member of them and not a primate over them.

Generally speaking, we do not see in the Book of Acts any trace of a special authority of the Apostle Peter over all the other apostles, but the opposite: we see that when the apostles met in Jerusalem to address the question of circumcision, they confessed the opinion of James, the brother of the Lord, not Peter's, and considered it an inspiration of the Holy Spirit. This is why they said in their conciliar decision: "it seemed good to the Holy Spirit" and added the words, "and to us" (Acts 15:28), openly confirming their mutual equality in rule and authority. Similarly, when it was needed to send one of the apostles to Samaria to confirm those who accepted therein the word of salvation, the apostles who were in Jerusalem sent them Peter and John (Acts 8:14). So, if Peter was a chief over all the apostles as the papists claim, would have they dared to choose the opinion of the Apostle James over his opinion, or send him with John to Samaria? And how would Peter himself have accepted that?

Also, if we carefully read the epistles of the apostles, we do not see in them any trace of primacy of the Apostle Peter over the rest of his brethren apostles, but on the contrary, we see that when the Apostle Paul first came to Jerusalem, after receiving the apostolic call in Damascus, he presented the Gospel that he preaches among the Gentiles not to Peter alone, but to all the apostles who were in Jerusalem at that time; these are: "James, Cephas (i.e. Peter), and John, who seemed (all three of them, with James in their forefront, not Peter) to be pillars [of the Church]" (Galatians 2:2-9). Then when Peter came to Antioch and started behaving with hypocrisy with the faithful among the Jews, the Apostle Paul did not hesitate to openly admonish him in front of everybody for not acting with straightness according to the truth of the Gospel (Galatians 2:11-21), which plainly indicates that first, the Apostle Peter was never a primate over the other apostles, otherwise the Apostle Paul, who was more recent than him and the other apostles in the

3. St. Peter's Relation to Other Apostles

apostolic call, would not dare to admonish him openly in front of everybody, and second, he was also not infallible, because infallibility belongs only to God, and if what the apostles wrote and taught is considered infallible, it is thus solely because it was by inspiration of the Holy Spirit. Not to mention that we see the Apostle Paul in his First Epistle to the Corinthians—who were divided among themselves, some of them ascribing themselves to Paul, others to Apollos and others to Peter, as if this or that apostle has an authority or reverence more than his other brethren apostles—admonishing them over that issue and showing them that all the apostles are equal to each other in service, teaching, authority, and reverence, and that the master of all, the head of all and the only foundation of the Church is the Lord Jesus Christ, to Whom only belongs all glory, reverence, and esteem (1 Corinthians 1, 3). Besides, the Apostle Peter in all his epistles calls himself brother and companion to all apostles and a participant in service with the rest of the Church shepherds and elders, and he warns all these shepherds and elders from rushing upon authority and governance, and he says that the only chief shepherd is the Lord Jesus Christ (see 1 Peter 5:1-4 and cf. 1 Peter 2:25 and 2 Peter 3:15).

We think that what we have set forth so far of the sayings of the Holy Fathers and the clear Biblical citations is sufficient to show the vanity of the first papist claims that the Apostle Peter was a primate over the apostles, or a head of the Church, or the only foundation of the Church.

St. Peter the Apostle (at St. Catherine's Monastery, Mt. Sinai)

PART 4

"Thou art Peter..."

But despite all this, if we assume again that there were rights for the Apostle Peter distinguished from his other brethren apostles, by what right do the popes of Rome ascribe them to themselves? Pope Leo XIII answers our question with the following expression: "But let them [the Eastern Orthodox] look back to the early years of their existence, let them consider the sentiments entertained by their forefathers, and examine what the oldest Traditions testify, and it will, indeed, become evident to them that Christ's Divine Utterance, 'Thou art Peter, and upon this rock I will build My Church,' has undoubtedly been realized in the Roman Pontiffs"![10] As for the meaning of this expression used by the pope, as it appears from the content of all his speech in the encyclical and from what the papists generally claim, is that the Lord Christ, by saying to the Apostle Peter, "thou art Peter, and on this rock I will build My church," made him the only foundation of the Church, thereby a primate over the rest of the apostles, and a vicar for Himself on earth. And since the Apostle Peter founded the church of Rome and remained its

---

10 Translator's note: Quotes in English from the encyclical are taken from the text obtained from this webpage: https://www.papalencyclicals.net/leo13/l13praec.htm

bishop for about twenty-five years, and finally received the crown of martyrdom in Rome, thus all those special rights he had were transferred after his death to his successors, the Roman bishops, by means of succession and inheritance! But this second claim of the papists is weaker than a spider web and contrary to the scriptural texts, the apostolic traditions, the ecclesiastic canons, the historical evidence, the teachings of the Church Fathers, and its early and late teachers because:

1. As we saw above, there is no lesser evidence neither in the Holy Scriptures nor in Holy Tradition that supports the papists' claim that the Apostle Peter is the only foundation of the Church, or that he was a primate over the rest of his brethren apostles, or a head of all the Church.

2. No lesser evidence or hint exists in the Holy Scriptures either about the residence of the Apostle Peter in Rome, or even about him going there, since there is clear evidence in the Scriptures that the Apostle Peter resided in Antioch (see Galatians 2:11). Yes, Holy Tradition says that the Apostle Peter was found worthy of the death of martyrdom in Rome, but the papists' claim that he also lived there more than twenty-five years, relying on what the two historians of the fourth century, Eusebius and Jerome, have recounted with neither scrutiny nor careful examination, is totally untrue. For if we carefully search the life of this apostle and his travels, we determine that it is impossible that he would have lived in Rome for more than one year by which end he was found worthy of the death of martyrdom.[11]

---

11 Aside from the Orthodox and Protestant historians, there exist several Western scholar historians and writers, such as Valesius, Pagi, Baluz, Hug, Klee, Döllinger, Waterworth, Allnatt and others (see "The Early Days Of Christianity" Part 2, Chapter 8, by the theologian, scholar and historian examiner, the English Farrar), who confess that the Apostle Peter did not live in Rome for more than one year. And in

3. In addition to being devoid of any basis in Scriptures and Holy Tradition, the papists' claim that the Apostle Peter was a bishop of the church of Rome is also inconsistent with the apostolic office of Peter, which is not a secret. For among the duties of the apostolic office, according to the witness of scriptures, is to spread the Christian faith <u>into all the world</u> (Mark 16:15) and preach the Gospel truths <u>to all the Gentiles</u> (Matthew 28:19 and Luke 24:47), not to reside as a simple bishop in one place over one nation. Furthermore, if Peter really lived in Rome for twenty-five years as a bishop of its church, would the Apostle Paul have dared to write

---

order that you, O Orthodox reader, double check the truth of our words, that the Apostle Peter did not reside in Rome for more than one year, contemplate what the Acts of the Apostles and the Epistles mention about this apostle and you will find that first, since the descent of the Holy Spirit on the apostles (year 33 A.D.) until the meeting of the apostles in Jerusalem to look into the matter of circumcision (year 50 A.D.), the Apostle Peter remained in Jerusalem and in the regions of Judea and Samaria. Second, when the Apostle Paul wrote his Epistle to the Romans (i.e. in year 58), Peter was not in Rome, otherwise Paul would have written him a greeting of peace at least. And third, when the Apostle Paul went to Rome and resided there two complete years (i.e. from year 60 until 62), Peter was not in Rome yet, otherwise he would have come with the brethren to receive Paul, or at least sent somebody from his part to receive him, or Paul himself, before summoning the leaders of the Jews in Rome and addressing them, would have gone to visit Peter. And should Peter have arrived to Rome before Paul, the leaders of the Jews would not have said to Paul that "any of the brethren who came reported or spoken any evil of you." Rather, if Peter was residing as the bishop over the Roman see for even one year or less before Paul's arrival to Rome, the leaders of the Jews would not have said to Paul, "we desire to hear from you what you think; for concerning this sect [Christianity], we know that it is spoken against everywhere" (see Acts 28:21-22). And if you add to all these years when Peter was not in Rome seven years he spent in Antioch and two or more years he spent preaching in Pontus, Galatia, Cappadocia, and Bithynia, then barely one year remains during which Peter resided in Rome at the end of his life.

to the people of this church a special epistle to teach and confirm them in the faith while the Apostle Peter was their bishop? And how come the Apostle Paul does not mention in his Epistle to the Romans at least a greeting of peace to its bishop the Apostle Peter while he mentions therein several greetings to several people, both men and women (see Romans 16)? Rather, we also see that the Apostle Paul does not bring any lesser mention or hint about the Apostle Peter in any of his many epistles about Rome, neither as its bishop nor as a preacher of its people.

4. If we carefully search the Holy Scriptures, we learn that the founder of the church of Rome is not the Apostle Peter, but the Apostle Paul, and it is more correct to say, "the disciples of the Apostle Paul" (see Romans 16). Then when Paul arrived to Rome, he confirmed the church founded by his disciples and remained preaching God's word therein also, and teaching its people the commandments of the Lord Jesus Christ for two complete years (see Acts 28:16-31). And yes, some of the fourth century writers attribute the founding of the church of Rome to the Apostle Peter; however, the correct tradition that is consistent with the scriptural evidence confirms that the founder of the church of Rome is the Apostle Paul, or both of the Apostles Paul and Peter together, who while still alive appointed three bishops at Rome—Paul appointed the first two bishops, Linus and Anacletus, while Peter appointed the third bishop, Clement—which also shows the invalidity of the papists' claim that the Apostle Peter was the first bishop of Rome.

5. Even if we consider to be true the tradition that the founder of the church of Rome is the Apostle Peter alone, this does not grant the bishops of Rome any lesser right to consider themselves alone to be Peter's

successors, because the Holy Scriptures witness and tradition confirms that the Apostle Peter founded by himself, or in collaboration with the Apostle Paul, other churches before founding the church of Rome, like the church of Antioch that is founded by both heads of the Apostles Peter and Paul, and the church of Alexandria that Peter alone founded and appointed its first bishop to be his beloved disciple Mark the Evangelist. So, in this case, the bishops of Antioch and Alexandria are worthier than the bishops of Rome to be called and be considered the successors of the Apostle Peter, especially the bishops of Antioch because clear evidence exists in Holy Scriptures as we saw previously (see Galatians 2:11) concerning the Apostle Peter going to Antioch and residing there, whereas concerning him residing in Rome or going there, there is no lesser clear evidence in Holy Scriptures. Hence, if there were special rights to the Apostle Peter as the papists claim, how was it concealed from Leo XIII's astute perception that those who are worthier of the rights of the Apostle Peter are not the bishops of Rome but the bishops of Antioch who are confessed, since ancient times, to be lawful successors of the Apostle Peter by all the Christian churches, even the church of Rome as well?

6. There is no doubt that the oldest and most revered Christian church is the church of Jerusalem that the Lord Jesus Christ Himself founded, therefore it is rightly called the "mother of churches." For in it the Holy Spirit descended on the Holy Apostles, and from it the Christian faith started to be spread to all nations; and to it the apostles used to come from their travels and meet to discuss the important religious and ecclesiastic issues; and on it the Lord Jesus Christ Himself, according to Holy Tradition, appointed the apostle James called the "brother of the Lord" as a bishop, not

to mention that in it also the great redemptive work of the Nativity of the Son of God and His teaching, passion, crucifixion, death, resurrection, appearance, and ascension took place; and in it John the Baptist the Forerunner of Christ was beheaded; and in it the Righteous Joseph, the betrothed of the Virgin Mary, reposed; and in it the Most Holy Theotokos lived her earthly life; and in it the Apostle James, Symeon of the seventy apostles, and Stephen (who was full of faith and the Holy Spirit) were worthy of the crown of martyrdom; and in it we have the cave, Golgotha, the Mount of Olives, the Garden of Gethsemane, the upper room of Zion, Thabor, Hermon, the Jordan River, and other miraculous events and holy places to which memory every knee and head bow and every mind marvels and every heart entreats.... So if there is truth in the claims of the bishops of Rome in the right of authority and primacy over all churches, are not the bishops of Jerusalem worthier of this right? And if the Lord Christ really wanted to make the Apostle Peter a primate over the rest of the apostles and a head of all the Church and His vicar on earth, would not He at least make him a bishop of Jerusalem, the mother of churches?

7. If we assume that the Apostle Peter has some authority over the rest of his brethren apostles, and that the bishops of Rome inherited from him this authority over all the Christian Church, is it rational to also assume that the remaining apostles who were still alive after the death of the Apostle Peter submitted to the authority of the bishops of Rome? We consider that there is not a rational person who can accept that the Apostle John, the beloved disciple of Christ, who was still alive after the death of the Apostle Peter for about thirty-five years, submitted to the bishop of Rome as

4. "Thou art Peter..."

the head of all the Christian Church as the papists claim contrary to Holy Scripture, Holy Tradition, and sound mind.

So from what is mentioned so far, according to the clear evidence from Holy Scripture, and Holy Tradition, and based on the given proofs and compelling arguments, it is clear that first, the Apostle Peter was not and could not be a primate over the rest of his brethren apostles because their primate, teacher, and lord was the Lord Jesus Christ Himself, neither a vicar for Christ nor a deputy for God on earth because no human can ever be a vicar or deputy for God Almighty. Hence the Lord Christ, before His salvific death, did not tell His disciples that He appointed or He will appoint Peter or another apostle as His vicar and deputy; rather He told them that He will send the Comforter, the Spirit of Truth i.e. the Holy Spirit "Who proceeds from the Father" Who will teach them everything and remind them of all that the Lord Jesus Christ told them (see Luke 14:26 and 15:26). Similarly, before His ascent into Heaven, He did not tell His disciples that He delivered or will deliver all authority in heaven and on earth to Peter or any other apostle, but He told them, "all authority has been given to Me in heaven and on earth," and promised them that He Himself will be with them (i.e. His Church) all the days until the end of times (see Matthew 28:18-20). And second, that the bishops of Rome are neither successors of the Apostle Peter because Peter did not found the church of Rome, nor the vicars of the Apostle Peter because Peter was not a bishop of Rome, nor heirs of some special rights of the Apostle Peter, first, because Peter never had such special rights at all as he was an apostle and servant of the Word, no more nor less, similar to the rest of his brethren apostles, and second, because if he had such rights, the bishops of Alexandria and Antioch are worthier of it, not the bishops of Rome.

St. Peter's Basilica, Vatican City

PART 5

The Vatican's Deceptive Historical Approach

But Pope Leo XIII, in addition to averting our gaze from what our fathers and forefathers thought and believed, strives to remind us, in his encyclical of altered and truncated historical events which he thinks support his claim, that the Eastern Orthodox Church, since ancient times until the schism, used to confess the primacy of the popes of Rome over all the Church! Here is what he says for this purpose: "The time, the reasons, the promoters of the unfortunate division [he means the schism between the Eastern and Western churches], are well known. Before the day when man separated what God had joined together, the name of the Apostolic See [he means the see of Rome as if it is the only apostolic see that exists] was held in Reverence by all the nations of the Christian world; and the East, like the West, agreed without hesitation in its obedience to the Pontiff of Rome, as the Legitimate Successor of St. Peter, and, therefore, the Vicar of Christ here on earth"! Then to support these sayings that are based on flattery and distortion, he mentions an event that he garnished with falsification and embellished with forgery. He says, "if we refer to the beginning of the dissension, we shall see that

Photius himself [for the reason that the Eastern church, based on the claim of the author of the encyclical, used to confess the primacy of the popes of Rome over all the Christian Church] was careful to send his advocates to Rome on the matters that concerned him [if you examine the books of all Eastern and Western historians, you will not find any trace of Photius sending advocates and mediators to Rome except him sending his peace letter to Pope Nicholas through the messengers of Emperor Michael, not his own messengers]; and Pope Nicholas I sent his Legates to Constantinople from the Eternal City, without the slightest opposition [Why not! As long as the popes, like the rest of the Eastern patriarchs, used to send their advocates by request of the emperor and the patriarchate of Constantinople to represent them in councils], 'in order to examine the case of Ignatius the Patriarch with all diligence, and to bring back to the Apostolic See a full and accurate report' [but why are you silent, O successor of Pius IX, on the consequence of the behavior of the two advocates of your predecessor Pope Nicholas, Radoald and Zacharias, who disregarded the vain commandment of their master, that is to leave the final judgment up to him in the question of Ignatius, but considered that, in accordance to the ecclesiastic canons and observed ancient customs, they left the final judgment to the council of bishops, not to the bishop of Rome alone, hence contrary to what Nicholas, the originator of the primacy heresy, confessed along with all council members the dismissal of Ignatius and electing Photius as patriarch instead, and they signed the acts of the council]; so that the history of the whole negotiation is a manifest [?] confirmation of the Primacy of the Roman See [!] with which [says the heinous claim of pope Nicholas in the right of primacy over all the church] the dissension [he means between the Eastern church and the Western church] then began"!

5. Vatican's Deceptive Historical Approach

Any person who has the least knowledge of correct church history who reads these expressions in the encyclical cannot help but be greatly perplexed not knowing what is more strange therein: is it the boldness of the encyclical's author in falsifying the historical events that are known to everybody, or the shabbiness of the papists' arguments in general in defending the primacy heresy? And if this papist encyclical was written for the students of papist schools, nobody would be surprised by the boldness of falsification of historical events or the shabbiness of arguments and proofs, because papist students are forced to accept every word coming from the mouth of the pope as obvious truth.

But this encyclical is composed for the "kings and all peoples;" therefore every lover of truth would have hoped to find in it carefully examined historical research for the truth of the differences between the Christian churches and for a fair inspection free of all intent and secluded from all trickery and blandishment when listing historical events. But what a disappointment! For the author of the encyclical thought that listing a truncated piece of those papist myths, that are garnished with enough fabrication, would convince the kings of the earth with its powers, peoples, and scholars with the correctness of his broad claim in the right of primacy over all the church! Alas to the poverty of the Vatican databases from honest evidences, rational references, crystal-clear truths, and brilliant luminaries, as long as Pope Leo XIII, at the end of our nineteenth century could not find in them a stronger proof or greater evidence to support his broad claim other than repeating what the papacy's assistants used to say and write during the dark barbaric ages, the Middle Ages, on the question of the two patriarchs Photius and Ignatius and their relation at that time with the pope of Rome Nicholas I! But it is enough to look at the correct history to confirm the vanity of all the statements of the author of the encyclical mentioned above.

Regarding what the author of the encyclical says, that all the Christians of the East before the schism confessed the primacy of the pope like the Christians of the West, we say based off the enacting terms of honest history that, since the broad claim of the bishops of Rome in the right of authority, rule, and primacy over all the Church, the Christians of the East as well as many of the Christians of the West have always rejected it as a claim that is contradictory to the spirit of Christian teachings, opposite to apostolic traditions, and inconsistent with the canons of ecumenical and local councils. Thus we see in the second century that the bishops of the church of Asia, led by the bishop of Smyrna, Saint Polycarp the disciple of the Apostle John, rejected the request of the bishop of Rome Anicetus at that time to change their habit in the celebration date of Pascha that they received from the Apostle John, and neither the bishop of Rome nor his successors could judge in this issue until the first ecumenical council was held and solved this issue with the authority of all the Church. Also in the third century, when the bishop of Rome Stephen sharply rejected the arrogant decision of two local councils in Africa in regards to baptizing the heretics reverting to Orthodoxy, and threatened to excommunicate all who disagree with his opinion claiming that he is a "bishop over the bishops," then Saint Cyprian Bishop of Carthage immediately summoned the council of African bishops (year 256) and said before them the following: "For neither does any of us set himself up as a bishop of bishops, nor by tyrannical terror does any compel his colleague to the necessity of obedience; since every bishop, according to the allowance of his liberty and power has his own proper right of judgment, and can no more be judged by another than he himself can judge another."[12] Then in his 71st letter he says: "For neither did Peter, whom first the Lord chose,

---

12 Translator's note: Quoted from: https://www.ccel.org/ccel/schaff/anf05.iv.vi.i.html

5. Vatican's Deceptive Historical Approach

and upon whom He built His Church, when Paul disputed with him afterwards about circumcision, claim anything to himself insolently, nor arrogantly assume anything; so as to say that he held the primacy, and that he ought rather to be obeyed by novices and those lately come."[13] In general, we see that there are several similar examples in history that clearly witness that the Church never confessed any authority or primacy of the bishops of Rome over all Christian churches, but on the contrary, it always rejected the claim of the contenders among them of such authority or primacy, and it never acknowledged them except the right in <u>primacy of honor</u> only which was granted to them by the second and fourth ecumenical councils, not considering that they are successors of the Apostle Peter, but considering that they are the bishops of the city of Rome, the capital of the Roman empire at that time. It also granted this right in primacy of honor to the bishops of Constantinople, the new capital of reign.[14] Accordingly, the right in primacy of honor that the Church granted to the bishop of Rome, the old capital of reign as well as the bishops of Constantinople, the new capital of reign, is a temporal right not based on Christian teachings nor apostolic traditions but solely on civil consideration. And if circumstances and situations sometimes forced some bishops and patriarchs of the East to seek brotherly help from the bishop of Rome to solve some issues and problems, this does not indicate at all that they confessed any primacy he has over them as perverted by Pope Leo XIII in his encyclical, because they used to seek his help as a brother seeks help from his brother, first, because he is detached from the machinations of the imperial royal court, and second, because he is the primate of honor

---

13 Translator's note: Quoted from: https://earlychurchtexts.com/public/cyprian_to_quintus_on_heretical_baptism.htm

14 See Canon 3 of the Second Ecumenical Council and Canon 28 of the Fourth Ecumenical Council.

among them, as much as the patriarchs of Alexandria, Antioch, and Jerusalem currently, when facing an important issue in their churches, seek the help of the patriarch of Constantinople who is the primate of honor among them, without him considering this action an indication of their confession of any authority over them at all.

And had the bishops of Rome preserved the dignity of their primacy of honor among the rest of their brethren bishops, the Eastern church would have always confessed this right and considered them the first among the Christian bishops, and that saddening schism between East and West would not have happened. But unfortunately the bishops of Rome changed this primacy of honor granted by the Church, considering their civil status, into that broad claim of the right of authority and primacy over all Christian churches, thereby, on the one hand, they were forced to support their claim in the right of primacy, to falsify scriptures, forge historical events, and fabricate false arguments known as Pseudo-Isidorian decretals; and on the other hand, they became a primary reason of the schism of the Church of Christ into Eastern and Western. And this is the reason why Patriarch Photius, after first seeking the brotherly help of the pope of Rome, began strongly rejecting the involvement of the pope in the matters of the Eastern church because his noetic discernment immediately showed him what could result from such uncanonical involvement of great danger on the freedom of the Church, especially since Pope Nicholas I was sitting on the papist throne at that time, whom contemporary historians, both Western and Eastern, regarded as a stubborn man, quick to anger, of fierce morals, rude, once-almighty, a lover of glory and haughtiness, and fond of authority and primacy, not only over all Christian churches but also over all kings and princes, as witnessed by his own words and actions. For among his words is what he wrote in one of his letters to

5. Vatican's Deceptive Historical Approach

Bishop Adventius where he says, "you submit to the ruler following the apostolic command, and this is right. But pay attention that these kings and rulers are true and legitimate. Carefully consider—do they rightly govern themselves and their followers? After all, the evil one cannot be beneficial by himself. Otherwise, you have to consider them as insurgents and resist them instead of submitting to them. So, submit to the king when he transcends you in virtues, not in vices, and for God's sake, as the apostle commanded, not contrary to God"! There is nothing better than what the famous Western historian Abbé Fleury said regarding these words of Pope Nicholas when he said, "The pope does not know that the emperor that the apostle commanded to obey at that time was Nero, and that the apostle himself commanded the slaves to obey their masters, not only the righteous ones but the wicked ones as well. And the pope made the bishops judges over the kings to rule—are these righteous or wicked? He even made all the flock judges over kings. Because the reason that the pope mentions encompasses everybody who must obey their kings."[15] And we say that the bishop of Rome has forgotten the words of the apostles to the Romans that every authority is from God, and he who resists the ruler resists God's institution, and those who resist bring judgment on themselves (Romans 13:1-2). The acts of this pope were not gentler than his words, for throughout all the term of his popery, he sometimes used to sow disputes, unrest, and wars among kings of Europe, and at other times he excommunicated kings, bishops, and councils. He selectively chose what to do through his delegates according to what benefited his own interests. He subjected all independent dioceses in the West to the throne of Rome, calling all who resist his will schismatics and excommunicating them. His pride even reached the point

---

15 See Fleury, *Histoire Ecclésiastique*, 50:34.

when he brought down Emperor Louis II from his horse and made him walk in front of him pulling the horse.[16]

Hence, how far are the words and acts of this mighty pope, whom Pope Leo XIII calls "the great Roman pontiff" (!), from the astounding words and blessed works of Patriarch Photius, to which all Western and Eastern scholars and historians have witnessed?[17] It suffices to mention his second letter to Pope Nicholas I that is filled with the spirit of Gospel love, Christian kindness, divine love, and love of peace between churches, which his enemies themselves still marvel at until now and call it a miracle. Therefore, what was the cause of the schism in this case: the kindness of Patriarch Photius and his Christian humility or the pride of Pope Nicholas and his demonic arrogance? To you we address this question, O "vicar of God on earth" Leo XIII, asking you to judge with justice and fairness, not with dishonesty and partiality....[18]

---

16 Among the Western historians see Regino of Prüm, "Chronicon," year 858, and the Jesuit monk Maimbourg, "History of the Schism of the Greeks," Paris, 1776. Among the Eastern historians see Amphilo 20, Footnote 4, and the history of Meletios 9:11 Number 3, and Dositheus 7:13 Number 3, and many others.

17 Among the Western historians see Fleury 50:3 and Pitzipios "On the Eastern Church" 1:4, Paris, 1855.

18 Those who, among the Arab Orthodox faithful, would like to know the real causes of the schism in detail are asked to read the books "The Rock of Doubt" and "The History of the Schism" by the Reverend priest Archimandrite Gerasimos Massarra. These causes are mentioned briefly in our translation of the booklet by the Reverend priest Basilios Mikhaelovsky entitled "A Historical View of the Papist Church Delusions", Kazan, 1894.

PART 6

Infallibility

But can Pope Leo XIII judge upon this issue contrary to what his predecessors ruled without touching on the dogma of "infallibility" confirmed by his predecessor Pius IX? Doubtlessly not. Actually, we see that Pope Leo XIII is not different at all from his predecessors when talking about this issue in his encyclical, but we also see him doubling down in distorting the correct historical report to affirm that the Greeks (he means the Eastern Orthodox), who were the reason of the schism according to his claim, confessed their mistake and consented to the high authority of the pontiffs of Rome in two great councils! And here is the expression in the encyclical: "Finally, in two great Councils, the second of Lyons and that of Florence, Latins and Greeks, as is notorious, easily agreed, and all unanimously proclaimed as Dogma the Supreme Power of the Roman Pontiffs"!

What made you, O "vicar of the apostle Peter," remind us of these two fabricated councils if your broad claim about the right of authority over all the church has lesser trace in Holy Scriptures or the canons of the Ecumenical Councils? Perhaps you are ignorant or you feign ignorance of the reasons of the convening of these two "great" councils according to your claim? And if the Greeks, i.e. Eastern

Christians (as you claim, and not some of them only as is true, who were not lead by the Eastern patriarchs, but by the Byzantine emperors because they were hoping to receive help from the West to block the attacks of external enemies, not because they believed in the primacy of the pontiffs of Rome), really confessed the primacy of the pope and united with the papist church, who are these Eastern Christians who you are calling now in your encyclical to unite and confess your authority, supremacy and primacy? But as long as the Eastern Christians even now still reject the primacy of the popes of Rome and refuse any communion with the papist church that is full of heresies and innovations, is this not a straight indication and clear proof that the primacy of the pope as dogma confessed in the councils mentioned by some clerics and laymen among the Eastern (for the former it was due to low self-respect or greed of bribery, and for the latter it was in hope of receiving help from the West through the pope against the enemies of the Byzantine nation) was nothing but a coercive external confession based on personal interest and not an internal voluntary confession based on a belief from the heart, thus that union was nothing but a false union based on fabrication and distortion, not on the pillars of honesty and truth? And if the Eastern [Christians] truly confessed the primacy of the pope at that time, as claimed by the author of the encyclical, why was the union between the two churches not established? Or perhaps Pope Leo XIII imagines that the Eastern [Christians] are ignorant and illiterate to the point they do not know the history of their church and what the popes of Rome committed against it of oppression, injustice, diverse aggression, legitimate and illegitimate means to submit it to their tyrannical authority? So, if he is ignorant and feigns ignorance of correct history, we Orthodox are not ignorant that the Eastern Church was not aware of the fabricated union that took place in the two councils mentioned. This

6. Infallibility

is why nobody among the Eastern [Christians] heeded the decision of the first council of Lyons, even Emperor Michael Paleologos himself, who, after being the first advocate for the decision of this council hoping to receive help from the West, and after being disappointed from receiving this help, soon rejected the decision of the council openly in front of all the people and banned the deacon from mentioning the name of the pope. In the second council in Florence, nobody accepted its decision except some of the Eastern [Christians] who attended after great efforts and the use of all sorts of trickery, promises and threats against them, not "easily" as the author of the encyclical claims, either out of ignorance or feigning ignorance of true history. As for the rest of the Eastern [Christians] who attended that unfortunate council, with Mark of Ephesus the champion of Orthodoxy at their forefront, they never accepted the decision of this council and did not sign it. As a witness to the invalidity of that council, it suffices to hear what Pope Eugenios IV at that time said when the Latins told him that Mark of Ephesus did not sign the council decision. He said, "Woe to us brethren, we did not accomplish anything." Indeed, the Latins did not accomplish anything despite all their trickery, quibbles, and promises, but they were disappointed and their hopes vanished, especially the hopes of "the successor of Peter," in submitting the Eastern Church to his authority through this fabricated council. This happened because as soon as the news of this council circulated among the Orthodox of the East, they all stood against it so that when those who signed the decision returned to Constantinople, they regretted what they did and started blaming themselves saying, "let the hand that signed be cut, and let the tongue that confessed be plucked out." Then following these events, many Orthodox councils convened in Jerusalem (year 1443 in the presence of the patriarchs of Alexandria, Antioch, and Jerusalem), Trebizond, Russia, Romania, Serbia, and

Georgia, and three councils in Constantinople (the last one was in 1450 during the times of the last Byzantine Emperor Constantine Paleologos). They all rejected the decree of the fabricated union and condemned the council of Florence as a robber (false) council. What a big difference between the perversions of the encyclical author and these historical truths. Would it not have been more appropriate for Pope Leo XIII to not remind us of these sad events that support the continuous efforts of the popes of Rome to impose their heavy yoke on the Eastern [Christians] similar to how they imposed it on the Western [Christians], and which memory increase the repulsion and abhorrence of the Orthodox from the papist church? Or perhaps he thinks that by merely telling the Orthodox (imitating the words of the Lord Jesus), "Come to Me, all you who labor and are heavy laden, and I will give you rest. Take My yoke upon you and learn from Me, for I am gentle and lowly in heart, and you will find rest for your souls," they will abandon their church freedom and apostolic teachings that they received from their fathers and are still firmly upholding for nineteen centuries and will hasten to bear the papist yoke of slavery on their necks? No, and never will we listen to your invitation, O Vaticanist father, no matter how arrogant you are, how haughty, how elevated, and how much you claim that you are "the vicar of Christ and the deputy of God on earth," because we Orthodox have never been accustomed to bearing a spiritual yoke other than the yoke of Christ our Heavenly Father and only Head of our Church, Who is the only One capable of bestowing upon us patience and comfort in our struggles to pluck out the tares of corrupt teachings and multiple machinations sown in the midst of the wheat of our correct Orthodox teachings, by your diverse sorts of workers: Jesuits, Franciscans, Dominicans, Capuchins, Lazarists, etc., who grow in the West like tiny seeds and soon spring up in the East like large plants.... But let us go back to the encyclical.

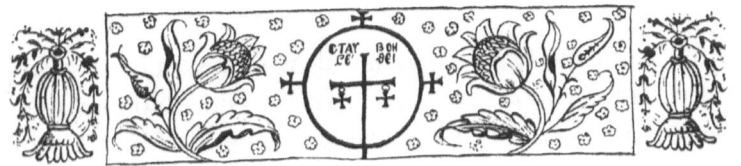

PART 7

The Pope's False Promises

It seems that Pope Leo XIII noticed that what he stated in his encyclical of distorted evidence, falsified proofs, and fabricated events to support his claim of the right of primacy over all the church cannot be accepted by the minds of the Orthodox. Hence, we see him abandoning the proofs and arguments and follows up with inviting them to the union through promises and commitments. This is what Pope Leo XIII promises in his encyclical, not only on his behalf, but also on behalf of all his successors! He says, "Nor is there any reason for you to fear on that account that We or any of Our successors will ever diminish your rights, the privileges of your Patriarchs, or the established Ritual of any one of your Churches." But does history confirm this saying of Pope Leo? If we carefully read history, we learn unfortunately that this saying of the pope is no more honest than his claim of the right in primacy. It suffices to remember the orders of his predecessors and the current efforts of his Jesuit workers in Syria to force our Greek Catholic, Maronite, and Syriac brethren to change their church rites and local customs, and gradually replace them with Latin rites and customs. Here is what was written on this topic by Mr. Lopukhin, a contemporary theology professor at the San Petersburg Theological Academy, in his response to the encyclical of Pope Leo XIII. He said, "Nobody reads these promises in the encyclical without exclaiming 'Credat Judaeus Apella, non ego' which means, let anybody who wishes believe it, except myself. For history presents us much solid evidence of the lies of these deceitful promises such that we cannot give it any lesser importance. It suffices to mention the usurping acts of the Latins in Western Russia toward the Russians living in Poland, who united with them, to wipe every trace of their Eastern rites, even their Russian citizenship as well. Moreover, the co-papists are still until now striving to convert the Russians in Galicia [a territory under the Austrian rule] into Latins. It seems to me that the Jesuits purposely deride and mock the promises of the encyclical, thus we see them seizing the Russian monasteries and churches in Galicia and transforming them into Latin churches and Polish monasteries! Is it with these events and measures occurring in front of our eyes and the eyes of all the world that the 'great vicar of God on earth' thinks that he convinces us in his promises?"[19]

If we honestly believe the will of this encyclical's author, and assume that his promises are true although experience and history have always denied them, why did Pope Leo XIII adhere to the issue of rites and customs and remain silent from mentioning the more important, that is the dogmas? Though we are glad to see the president of the Catholic world publicly confessing the truth of our Orthodox church teachings, as he says, "in defense of the Catholic Faith, we often have recourse to reasons and testimony borrowed from the teaching, the Rites, and Customs of the East." Good, but why does he not mention anything in his encyclical about the innovative teachings of his papist church such as the addition to the Creed, indulgences, the purgatory fires, papal

---

19 See *The Ecclesiastic Preacher* magazine, Number 29-31, year 1894, in Russian.

7. The Pope's False Promises

infallibility, the immaculate conception of the Theotokos, and many other dogmas and teachings that are contrary to the spirit of our Orthodox Church? If the pope thinks, by being silent on these papist teachings in his encyclical by which he invites us to the union, that if we confess his only demand, the dogma of primacy, we will be obliged to gradually confess the rest of the papist dogmas that are nothing but a natural consequence of the primacy dogma, the source of all heresies and innovations in the Western church, we declare to him his disappointment with us, for if we Orthodox do not agree with any slight change in our rites and customs, much more we will never agree with any slight change in the dogmas. Even if we also assume that the pope will leave our rites and customs alone as well as our teachings and dogmas and expect our confession of his primacy only, despite this, we cannot accept the union with a church full of heresies and innovations that are contrary to the teachings of our Orthodox Church. And no matter how much he speaks words of flattery and fatherly love, far be it from him to be able to fulfill the hidden desires of his heart, especially since the history of some of the Eastern denominations that united with the papist church clearly showed us that the filial obedience that the "Vaticanist father" is asking from us now is more horrible than all slavery, because he asks to enslave not our bodies but our souls in order to deprive it from religious freedom. Is there a slavery more repulsive than this slavery?

Baptism of Rus (grayscale), Mikhail Shankov (2003)

PART 8

The Pope's Lofty Promises

We wonder, what does Pope Leo XIII promise us in return for his great request from us, i.e. in return for our submission to his papal authority? He promises us all earthly and heavenly goods! And this is what he says, "if you re-establish Union with us [i.e. if we confess the authority of the pope and unite with the papist church], you will see how, by God's bounty, the glory and dignity of your Churches will be remarkably increased." Then when addressing the Slavic Orthodox people, he promises them other greater goods as he says, "the [papist] church is anxious to welcome you also to her arms, that she may give you manifold aids to salvation, prosperity, and grandeur"! So, as you see, O reader, the pope promises great goods "of different colors and shapes" as we say in our spoken Arabic language, that is with honor, order, salvation, prosperity, and grandeur (and we cannot hide our astonishment from the grandeur of the "vicar of God on earth" who promises the Slavic people all the earthly and heavenly goods while he promises the remaining Orthodox people only some earthly goods! Does he perhaps think of us, relative to the Slavs, as nothing more than peasants, and that the peasant is satisfied with an onion? May God forgive him for this insult whether voluntary or involuntary), but unfortunately, he does not present us any lesser guarantee or warranty to receive these goods. Yes, we do not deny the greatness of the power of Pope Leo XIII in most of the Catholic world, along with the richness of his Vaticanist treasures, and the large number of his messengers who travel land and sea to win one proselyte, and when they win him, they make him twice as much a son of hell as themselves. But despite all this, how can the pope grant us all the goods he promises us, while with all that great power he has, we see that he cannot grant even a portion of it to the children of his papist church in the West, who suffer from the oppression of their wealthy brethren (not to mention that he himself often complains and weeps due to his afflictions and the aggression of his children toward his rights and authority)? Where is his royal dominance while his closest children, i.e. the Italians, have seized his properties and deprived him from his temporal power? Where is his papal authority while the greatest Catholic kingdom, i.e. France, has expelled his name and the name of papacy from its secular schools? Where is his ecclesiastic power or his spiritual primacy while the prime minister of a Catholic nation, such as Hungary, has stepped over his papal rights and transformed the great mystery of marriage to a political game? And what do we say about the freemasons, Mormons, materialists, socialists, anarchists, and nihilists, whose numbers are increasing day after day in most Catholic kingdoms and countries? So, can we Eastern Orthodox hope in this case for a reformation or success from one who is incapable of reforming his condition or improving the condition of the children of his own church? Rather, why do we need union with the papist church as long as this union does not bring us any spiritual or moral benefit, not to mention that it threatens our religious freedom, our Orthodox dogmas, our noble ecclesiastic rites and our ancient local customs? "No! It is not us who need the help of the pope, but he needs our help. For his sense of degeneration in the West made him ask to himself for a slave in the form of an ally in the East."[20]

---

20 See the response to the encyclical by the brilliant writer Mr. Kireyev, page 25, Petersburg, year 1895.

PART 9

Papal Administration

Let no one imagine that we hold the spirit of fanaticism or the hatred of peace toward the divided Christian churches and their union. On the contrary, the spirit of peace, love, and unity is the spirit of the Orthodox Church, and it spreads it in the hearts and minds of its children from their youth through its Christian teachings and daily and nightly prayers. But we cannot accept a false union such as the one presented to us by Pope Leo XIII, because history has taught us and experience confirms the invalidity of every union with the papist church, who insists on its heresies and innovations that are contrary to the spirit of the Orthodox Church (especially the papal primacy heresy that is the origin of all evils, the source of all heresies, and the reason of the original schism). Even if we assume that the pope pledges to abandon all the innovated papist teachings and dogmas except the primacy dogma, despite that, we cannot unite with the papist church under this heavy condition, i.e. confessing the absolute papal primacy over all the Christian churches.

For in addition to the absence of any basis of this primacy, as we saw, neither in Holy Scripture, nor in Holy Tradition, nor in the canons of the ecumenical councils, nor in the writings of the Holy Church Fathers, it is also opposed to the steadfast approach of the internal and external order of administration in our Orthodox church that is based on the principles of freedom, equality, and evangelical fraternity that are followed since the ancient Christian ages. Actually, if we examine the order of our Orthodox churches, we see that despite its composition of different people and several languages, i.e. Arabs, Greeks, Serbs, Bulgarians, Russians, Romanians, Georgians, Albanians, Mongols, Japanese, Indians, and Americans, each of these peoples forms a local church independent from the rest of its brethren in language, race, and internal administration, but is firmly connected to them in the bond of the one Orthodox Faith and in the unity of dogmas, rites, and customs observed since ancient times, without any difference or discrepancy, and they all form the members of one Body whose only Head is our Lord and God Jesus Christ. And since the Orthodox Church is far from every worldly spirit, consistent with the commandment of its Divine Head that orders to render to Caesar the things that are Caesar's and to God the things that are God's, we see that it is able to live in full accordance and union with governors and rulers in any kingdom and under any regime, whether royal or republican, absolute or bounded, Christian or non-Christian, Orthodox or heterodox, while papism, given its requirement to be exalted above every spiritual and temporal authority and rule, cannot live in comfort and accord not even with the Catholic kingdoms as is the case currently in the Western countries. For if the Orthodox churches wished in this case to submit to the papal authority, they would lose their mystical order and unique organization, and each one of these churches would become nothing more than an inferior diocese subordinate to the throne of Rome and subject to the whims of the Vatican pontiff.

Moreover, their patriarchs, councils, and hierarchs would become puppets in the hands of the pope's delegates

9. Papal Administration

and his Latin messengers, Jesuits, Franciscans, Dominicans, and Capuchins, as is the case currently with the patriarchs and bishops of our Catholic, Maronite, Syriac, Armenian, and Chaldean brethren who are incapable of making any move without the Latin monks, especially the Jesuits who openly restricted almost all education of boys and girls, and all national clergy who are subject to the papal throne, to their control. So, if there was any hint of sincerity in the sayings of "the blessed successor of Peter," that the apostolic papal throne always permits those who submit to it to keep their church rites and local customs, what is his purpose then in sending groups of Western monks to the East, who are come from foreign lands and speak a foreign tongue, who spare no effort nor miss any means to introduce the Latin church teachings and strange customs to the churches who are united, rather, enslaved, to the papist church, as confirmed by the patriarchs of these churches themselves who established the arguments against these monks in the council that convened in Rome to discuss that union? And if the trickery of the "Vatican prisoner" worked on those non-Orthodox "Eastern patriarchs," since he issued a decree in this council that forbids his Latin monks from meddling in the issues of the churches of the East that are in submission to the papal throne and only permits them in taking care of the schools, does he think that it will work on us Orthodox who were taught by history and experience that the nationals who are raised in the schools of Latin monks become more Latin than the Latins themselves? Not to mention that if the pope considers the patriarch a patriarch and the bishop a bishop in the denominations that are united with the papist church, why does he need to appoint bishops, especially Latin patriarchs, among these Eastern Catholic denominations? And if he says that appointing these Latin patriarchs is necessary in order to fulfill the needs of his Western fellows who live in the East,

Austrians, French, Italians, etc., and not to impose orders and prohibitions among the nationals and constrain the freedom of local patriarchs, we answer that if these Latin laity, whose number does not exceed one thousand souls throughout all Syria and Palestine, do not wish to submit to the local Catholic clergy (although this contradicts the meaning of union), they can fulfill their spiritual needs according to their Latin rites with the Jesuit, Franciscan, Dominican, or Capuchin fathers who outnumber them. Or if the monastic canons of these "ascetics in the world" fathers do not allow them to fulfill the spiritual needs of the laity, was it not more appropriate for the pope to send Latin priests, not patriarchs or bishops, at least in consideration of the local patriarchs and bishops, and in reverence to the canons of the apostles and the ecumenical councils that do not allow the existence of two bishops in one archdiocese?

Hence, what is the point of the existence of a Latin patriarch in Jerusalem when the local Catholics there have a national patriarch? And what is the point of that union between the Eastern Catholic churches in Syria and the papist church when each of these churches has its own patriarch, and each of these patriarchs calls himself an Antiochian patriarch? Who, perhaps, among these Antiochian patriarchs should be considered the true successor of the Apostle Peter on the Antiochian throne: the patriarch of the Maronites, or the patriarch of the Greek Catholics, or the patriarch of the Syriac Catholics, or the patriarch of the Chaldean Catholics, or the patriarch of the Armenian Catholics, or the patriarch of the Latins who lives in the Vatican? Among the strange things in the situation of these Catholic patriarchs is that some of them, such as the patriarch of the Greek Catholics for example, considers himself a patriarch, not only on the see of Antioch, but also on the see of Alexandria and the see of Jerusalem, contrary to the apostolic canons that do not allow the existence of one bishop in two archdioceses,

9. Papal Administration

how about him sitting on three apostolic sees? Even more strange is that this patriarch who is sitting on three apostolic sees is in submission with his three sees to the see of Rome! And what exceeds all strangeness is that this extent of lust of power has blinded the pontiffs of Rome such that they have reached a stage where they do not consider the essential Christian dogmas as important as the dogma of primacy; hence we see them accepting any sect in communion with the papist church, even if it was a heretical sect—it suffices that this sect confesses the primacy of the pontiff of Rome! How many denominations and Eastern churches who are now united with the papist church contradict each other in the most important Christian dogmas, in addition to their differences in church rites and customs? For some of them believe in the two natures while others believe in one nature; some believe in the two wills while others believe in the one will; some believe in the addition to the Creed while others reject this addition; some allow using unleavened bread while others loath its use; some of them allow the marriage of priests while others forbid it; some build their temples toward the East while others build them toward the West; and other dogmatic contradictions and ritual differences that are opposite to the spirit of true Christian unity.

But why should we further elaborate on this matter? For what we have mentioned suffices as fair evidence to the truth of our saying that the confession of the papal primacy, that Pope Leo XIII considers in his encyclical among the most important conditions of the union, is more repugnant and abominable than all bondage and slavery.

St. Gregory the Great of Rome

PART 10

Response of Pope Gregory the Great to Patriarch John the Faster

Pope Leo XIII could have saved us the labor of this response and sufficed himself, in his middle age, the burden of writing, the struggle of composition, and the hardship of repeating sophist claims that were previously debunked and rebutted by both Eastern and Western, if he at least remembered what one of his predecessors, Saint Gregory the Great, Pope of Rome, wrote in one of his letters to the patriarchs of Constantinople and Alexandria, to the emperor of Byzantium, and to others, against the lust for authority and primacy. For the sake of interest, we state here some of what that holy pope said in this regard in his letters. Hopefully Pope Leo XIII attends to it as well, benefits from it, and abandons his attachment to the primacy heresy, the origin of all papist delusions.

First, in his letter to the Patriarch of Constantinople John the Faster, who was the first to call himself "ecumenical," [Saint Gregory] says to him regarding this title: "Carefully consider that the peace of the Church is troubled because of your irrational haughtiness [what would this holy pope have said if he saw the true haughtiness of his successors; rather, what would he have written if he read the encyclical of Pope Leo XIII who calls himself in it 'the great vicar of God on earth'?]. From all your heart, love humility through which the love of the brethren and the unity of the Holy Ecumenical Church can be preserved. For when the Apostle Paul heard some say, 'I am of Paul, I am of Apollos, I am of Cephas,' he was troubled by tearing the Body of the Lord apart, and by the establishment of his members on foreign heads, and he cried, 'Was Paul crucified for you, or were you baptized in the name of Paul?' Thus the apostle avoided submitting the members of the Lord's Body to other than Christ, not even to the apostles themselves [how different are the words of this holy pope from the words of Pope Leo XIII?]. What do you say to Christ, <u>the ecumenical head of the Church</u> [rather what do you say, O 'Vaticanist father,' about these words of your predecessor? Is it truth? Or...?], on the terrible day of judgment: do you who by taking the title 'ecumenical' strive to submit all His members to yourself? Who are you following, by assuming this corrupt title, except the one who disdained the choirs of angels associated with him and strove to exalt himself above unity such that he does not submit to anybody and to appear higher than all [how dreadful is this reprimand that can be addressed now outright to the popes of Rome who claim the right of authority and primacy over all their brethren bishops!]? Yes, the Apostle Peter is truly the first member [not the head] of the Holy Ecumenical Church, but who are Paul, Andrew, and John? Are they not heads of specific people? Despite all this, they are all <u>members of the Church under the One Head</u>. In brief, I say that all the saints who are before the law, the saints who are under the law, and the saints who are under the grace constitute the Body of the Lord and are counted with the members of the Church, and none of them ever wished to be called ecumenical. Let your holiness know therefore that you exalt yourself when you wish to be called by a name that none of those true saints

10. Response of Pope Gregory

assumed to themselves. Are you ignorant that the hierarchs of this apostolic see that I serve in, by God's will, used to be called in the holy Chalcedonian council ecumenical solely for the sake of honor [here Saint Gregory the Great, the Pope of Rome, permits the use of the title 'ecumenical' if it was not for the sake of authority and governance over all the ecumenical church, but only for the sake of honor, as the Eastern Orthodox church considers it when it calls the patriarchs of Constantinople ecumenical]? Lo the church is currently being divided because of this prideful title and the hearts of all the brethren are troubled with doubts."[21]

Second, in his letter to Eulogios the Patriarch of Alexandria, he says the following concerning this title: "Even though the apostles are many, only one throne, I mean the throne of the preeminent of the apostles, is distinguished because of this preeminence due to its importance. This throne is peculiar to one in three locations [not only in Rome]. For he himself [the apostle Peter] revered the see [of Rome] where he reposed and lived his temporal life. He himself adorned the see [of Alexandria] to which he sent his evangelist disciple [Mark]. He himself also established the see [of Antioch] where he first presided for seven years. Accordingly, if the see that is now presided, with divine authority, by three bishops [of Antioch, Alexandria and Rome] is <u>one and for one</u>, I ascribe to myself all good things I hear about you, and ascribe all good things you yourself hear about me to your merits, <u>for we are all one</u> in the One who said: 'that they all may be one, as the Father [is] in Me, and I in [the Father]; that they also may be one in Us' (John 17)."[22]

As for his letter to the Byzantine Emperor Maurice, he says, "I dare to say that everyone who is called, or demands to be called, an ecumenical bishop, then with this haughtiness,

---

21 See Epistles of Saint Gregory the Great, Book 5, Letter 18.
22 See Epistles of Saint Gregory the Great, Book 7, Letter 40.

he makes himself a forerunner of the Antichrist [this is truly a bold saying but it now accurately applies to the popes of Rome who ask by word and deed to make themselves ecumenical bishops, not to mention that they claim what is more repulsive than this, that they are deputies of Christ and vicars of God on earth!]."[23]

This is what Saint Gregory the Great, Pope of Rome, believed and taught, although he was not less zealous than his predecessors and successors on the grandeur and importance of the throne of Rome, and we stated it here for no other reason than to remind his current successor Pope Leo XIII, whom we also address with the same words of this holy predecessor, of his saying: "I write this not against you but for you, because I cannot favor anybody over the Gospel commandments and church canons."[24]

St. John the Faster,
Patriarch of Constantinople

---

23   See Epistles of Saint Gregory the Great, Book 7, Letter 33.
24   See Epistles of Saint Gregory the Great, Book 5, Letter 18.

PART 11

The West's Corrupting Influence

This is what we perceived to write as a response to the encyclical of Pope Leo XIII, by which he addresses our Eastern Orthodox Church. While we confess that we fall short compared to what has been written and what will be written by the glorious and blessed scholars of our Church, we think that it is sufficient to carefully examine the call of Pope Leo XIII. Therefore, we end our response with the conclusion of the letter written last year by Anastasios Diomidis Kyriakos (1843–1923), professor of theology at the University of Athens, before the appearance of the encyclical of Pope Leo XIII, where he seems to foreknow what is coming in this encyclical in terms of empty claims that are, for a long time, known to everybody. He said, "Finally, wherever papism reigns, there is also spiritual, moral, literary, and intellectual corruption, as witnessed by true history and confirmed by daily experience. Actually, where did the greatest and most notorious enemies of the Christian religion appear—was it not in the Catholic country of France, the nation of Voltaire the chief among the atheists? Yes, we do not deny the existence of corruption in the Protestant countries such as England, Germany, Switzerland, and the Netherlands, as well as in Orthodox countries such as Greece and other Eastern countries. For surely, wherever there are humans, there is corruption, and no matter how strong the Christian religion is, it is unable to transform groups of humans to groups of angels. But in all cases, the corruption of Catholic people, such as the French, Italians, Spanish, Portuguese, South Americans, especially in Paris, Rome, Madrid, and Napoli, exceeds the level of extravagance and immoderation. This is also one of the reasons why the people of the East constantly reject any submission to the papal authority. Thus, it is the duty of the bishops of Rome in this case to understand this matter well, and spare us, from now on, the recitation of their many encyclicals, their diverse invitations, their broad claims, and their instigation for the union of the churches i.e. subjection of the Eastern church to the Western church. We have expressed our view quite often, and we now also say that as long as the people of the East remain of sound mind, it is impossible for them to walk in the road that leads to Rome, no matter how many times the sun turns around and the nights follow the days."

No matter how long they take, ages are short like a sun that rises then quickly sets.

Composed at the Theological Academy
in the God-protected city of Kazan
in the month of December
of the year 1894 A.D.

11. The West's Corrupting Influence

Anastasios Diomidis Kyriakos (1896)

UNCUT MOUNTAIN PRESS TITLES

Books by Archpriest Peter Heers

Fr. Peter Heers, *The Ecclesiological Renovation of Vatican II: An Orthodox Examination of Rome's Ecumenical Theology Regarding Baptism and the Church*, 2015

Fr. Peter Heers, *The Missionary Origins of Modern Ecumenism: Milestones Leading up to 1920*, 2007

Fr. Peter Heers, *Formation in the Love of Truth*, 2024

The Works of our Father Among the Saints, Nikodemos the Hagiorite

Vol. 1: *Exomologetarion: A Manual of Confession*
Vol. 2: *Concerning Frequent Communion of the Immaculate Mysteries of Christ*
Vol. 3: *Confession of Faith*

The Works of our Father Among the Saints, St. Hilarion (Troitsky)

Vol. 1: *On the Dogma of the Church: An Historical Overview of the Sources of Ecclesiology*

The Works of our Father Among the Saints, St. Raphael of Brooklyn

Vol. 1: *In Defense of St. Cyprian*
Vol. 2: *On the Steadfastness of the Orthodox Church*

Other Available Titles

St. Gregory Palamas, *Apodictic Treatises on the Procession of the Holy Spirit*
Elder Cleopa of Romania, *The Truth of our Faith*
Elder Cleopa of Romania, *The Truth of our Faith, Vol. II*
Fr. John Romanides, *Patristic Theology: The University Lectures of Fr. John Romanides*
Demetrios Aslanidis and Monk Damascene Grigoriatis, *Apostle to Zaire: The Life and Legacy of Blessed Father Cosmas of Grigoriou*
Protopresbyter Anastasios Gotsopoulos, *On Common Prayer with the Heterodox According to the Canons of the Church*
Robert Spencer, *The Church and the Pope*
G. M. Davis, *Antichrist: The Fulfillment of Globalization*
Athonite Fathers of the 20th Century, Vol. I

Fr. Alexander Webster and Fr. Peter Heers, Editors, *Let No One Fear Death*
Subdeacon Nektarios Harrison, *Metropolitan Philaret of New York*
Elder George of Grigoriou, *Catholicism in the Light of Orthodoxy*
Archimandrite Ephraim Triandaphillopoulos, *Noetic Prayer as the Basis of Mission and the Struggle Against Heresy*
Dr. Nicholas Baldimtsis, *Life and Witness of St. Iakovos of Evia*
On the Reception of the Heterodox into the Orthodox Church: The Patristic Consensus and Criteria
Patrick (Craig) Truglia, *The Rise and Fall of the Papacy*
The Divine Service of the Eighth Œcumenical Council
The Orthodox Patristic Witness Concerning Catholicism
Hieromartyr Seraphim (Zvezdinsky), *Homilies on the Divine Liturgy*
Abbe Guettée, *The Papacy*
Fr. George Metallinos, *I Confess One Baptism*
Acts of the Eighth Œcumenical Council

Select Forthcoming Titles

George (Pachymeres), *Errors of the Latins* (2 volumes)
St. Hilarion (Troitsky), *Bible, Church, History: A Theological Examiniation*
Cell of the Resurrection, Mount Athos, *On the Mystery of Christ: An Athonite Catechism*
Fr. Theodore Zisis, *Kollyvadica*
St. Maximus the Confessor, *Opuscula: Theological and Polemical Works*
Fr. Peter Heers, *Going Deeper in the Spiritual Life*
Fr. Peter Heers, *On the Body of Christ and Baptism*
Athonite Fathers of the 20th Century, Vol. II

This 1ˢᵗ Edition of

UNION WITH ROME?

REFUTING THE ENCYCLICAL OF POPE LEO XIII written by Saint Raphael, Bishop of Brooklyn, typeset in Baskerville, and printed in this two thousand and twenty fifth year of our Lord's Holy Incarnation is one of the many fine titles available from Uncut Mountain Press, translators and publishers of Orthodox Christian theological and spiritual literature. Find the book you are looking for at

uncutmountainpress.com

**GLORY BE TO GOD
FOR ALL THINGS**

AMEN.

www.ingramcontent.com/pod-product-compliance
Lightning Source LLC
Chambersburg PA
CBHW021627080526
44585CB00013BA/941